MW00437151

EYE

Mike Bove

SPUYTEN DUYVIL
New York City

© 2023 Mike Bove
ISBN 978-1-959556-80-0

Library of Congress Control Number: 2023945255

for Lauren

CONTENTS

I.

Sight   3
Snow All Day   4
Emily Dickinson Upstairs   6
Borderland   7
Time's House   10
City by the Sea   11
Field Guide to Roadside Geology   12
Eye Land   14
One Plus One   15
Get Down   16
Lakes and Ponds   17
First Person   18
My Father's Retirement Party   22
Plow Drivers   23
Arrival   25
Mourning Dove   27
Out   28

II.

Thundersnow   31

Outage   32

Clarity   34

Mice in the Attic   36

Tree   37

Spin Cycle   39

Walking at Night   40

Anxiety in General   41

Buried / Unburied   46

While Hiking the Flatirons   48

The Storm's End Is Compared to a Death   50

Empty Churches   51

A Boy Implores   52

This Poem Isn't Going to Write Itself   53

First Loss   54

Eye of the Storm   56

Montaigne   58

III.

Eye of the Mind   63

In a Box of Old Toys   65

Cannonball   66

Cemetery in Winter   67

Night Manager   68

Who's There?   70

Clean Dark   71

What Doesn't Break You Makes You Stronger   72

Don't Make Any Major Decisions in March   73

Lifetime of Things   75

Warming Hours   76

Winter Thinks of Spring   77

Painted Tigers   78

Push Start   80

Snow   81

Momentary Quiet   82

Visit the Creek in Winter   84

The southern coast could get more than a foot of snow. This would make it the biggest storm for the Portland area in years.

— *Portland Press Herald*, March 3, 2023

Imagination doesn't create.
It sees connections to what is already there.

— Charles Simic

I.

SIGHT

a closed eye
sees just as well

as one that is open
and maybe

better maybe
more

Snow All Day

hour after hour
since waking

the storm comes
to pile and bury

and now
all outside
is sugar-shook

at the window
the eye
can gorge all day

birds swing
back and forth

their bodies
airborne and beautiful

they drop into
the mounds

transform into twitch

scratch secrets
in the snow

Emily Dickinson Upstairs

that morning she returned
to amherst after weeks
in cambridge where
she'd been for eye treatment
some mysterious ailment
which clouded and obscured
and caused her such pain
not just the eyes the fear
she'd never read again

can you imagine
that morning by the window
in her upstairs room
where she'd brought her favorite
volume held it close
eyelids closed breathless
to finally know and oh
the triumph of light
when the words did appear
and she spoke them out
in that sun-bright room where
sight had turned to song

BORDERLAND

eye
know my father

my father loved

us

and the mountains
in the west
near the state line

eye
see him
driving a red
station wagon
to the office

he was happy
holding sea glass
to the sun

when he was
angry

eye
was afraid
of his

silence

when he got old
eye
understood

better
who he'd been
and why he
loved

and who

when he died
eye
held his hand

and

looked at the clock
to remember
the time

but

eye
can't remember
anything

but

his palm

still
and warm
and the room
empty

he was gone
and silent

but

eye
wasn't anymore
afraid

TIME'S HOUSE

think when it snows like this
of those abandoned houses
off route 26
their doors frozen ajar
their windows smashed
someone
up and left and now
the occupant is time
pacing as a dim shifting shadow
or a piercing wind
hosting a reunion
for the drifts
who arrive slowly
through shattered panes
and throughout the night
fill every empty seat

City by the Sea

the only god left
in this town
is the ocean

the others
didn't last
through the first
hard winter
in their clean
delicate robes

the ocean
gives back all
you offer

which is more
than you can say
of other gods

Field Guide to Roadside Geology

it doesn't take much as evidenced by
the unseen stone waiting in the parking lot
of the grocery store where my mother
pushed me standing in the cart until
one of the wheels found that pebble
and the world stopped abrupt
but not my body falling toward asphalt
downward downward where all things go
my poor little self that once knew freedom
thereafter broken

a rock hammer in my hand
and one in my brother's and
we've been brought to the mountains
those western mountains adored
by my father where he knew a man
who owned a mine for tourmaline mostly
but also amethyst beryl and
quartz both smoky and rose
we cut the earth under the sun
and what more to say except
when we pulled a few crystals
and rinsed them in a pond
they were sparkle-wet and gleaming

and though we didn't know it then
that was one way my father loved

after heavy rain on our street
it was easy to make my body
flat in the road and push my fingers
through deposits left by
channels of water racing for the drain
in the midday sun my fingers ran
back and forth over the grains
giving them a life in light
and color bright gold and sheen
and orange with here and there a blue
with time my hand began
to dissolve don't ask me how
and if you watched you'd see a boy
prone in the road brushing sand
but not what he actually was
a boy who found treasure
jewels and a spark a fire
and light he made himself
and was from then on awash
in riches

EYE LAND

no doubt there's truth
to say not one of us is
an island but also true
to say each of us is

islands are worlds
by themselves as we are
yet connected to land
beneath the sea

there's hope in believing
we can be close again
when the tide goes out
if only we'd let it

ONE PLUS ONE

imagine
my parents' joy
in the early days
when they discovered
their birthdays were
just a day apart
hers on the first
his on the second
did they note then
the significance of
those dates and how two
comes naturally from one
it's good to think of them
laughing in that
undivided togetherness
when or just before
they learned they
were in love

GET DOWN

with the wind like this
every spindly tree
in the maple grove is
swaying
leafless arms outstretched
and stick fingers barely
brushing their partners'
before getting swept
by the next groove
it's a woodland soirée
a deciduous two-step
and the wind sets
the tempo to arhythmic
shuffle and who cares
that no one else
can hear it
just because
they can't
doesn't mean
it's not music

LAKES AND PONDS

winter is not the only time
for considering mortality

but bare trees and frozen
streams make it easy

the local news reports
a record number of people

falling through ice
on lakes and ponds

too warm this year
and maybe next

too many reminders
of the inevitable

we make our way
soft-stepping slowly

though things look safe
our lives here are glass

First Person

1.
was it you
eye saw
my first day
and was it me
you waited for
like an emissary
from a better place
with a message of hope
in the shape of a cry
you kept me warm
you kept me
as best you could

2.
eye alone
alone in the house
alone with you
you alone
you asleep and me
alone
what had you done
to sleep so much
what made you
so tired eye
won't ever know

3.
there was always
one thing
eye wanted eye
wanted only for you
to be awake
and alright and to stop
drinking
at night hiding
around the house
hiding to drink
and it's true you are
without control
it's not my fault
you used to say
it's not your fault
is true
and not mine
is also true

4.
angry
at what you were
and greatly ashamed
until it was known

your shame was
so large and so much
it couldn't possibly
fit inside the child
eye was

5.
don't be afraid
of it is what we should say
each day when
we remember
don't be afraid of a life
already mostly lived
there may not be anything
left to do except
to not any longer
be afraid

6.
will it be me
the last one you see
on your last day
the day you may have
wanted for so long
it may not be me

it just may not be
but even if not
it will
it will

My Father's Retirement Party

in a photo
from that night
my parents are dancing
their hands together
their smiles wide
but what of those eyes
red from the flash
as if some future fire
was starting
even then
to burn

PLOW DRIVERS

drivers know the rig

know that with this
lever pulled
or button pressed
an angel's wing of steel
descends to the road
in the sacred name of
clearing and passage

drivers weave down
narrow streets between
parked cars
and last week's trash
hands on the wheel and feet
on the pedal

thought has no place

their minds
see it happening
because it's happened
a thousand times before

drivers know
a simple truth

when you've worked
a machine this long
and want to
clear the way
all you need is
fuel and faith
and one more
thoughtless day

ARRIVAL

eye

remember now

the days they were
born
and both could fit
inside my arms

eye oh eye

could sing no songs
no song eye knew
no guide no rules

and yet

my promise
from those days on

a promise
whispered
without sound

no shame
no fear
no cold regret

we make
our own
way now

Mourning Dove

as children
we thought
they were
morning doves
not mourning
and until we learned
we thought their call
signaled beginnings

in adulthood
we thought only of
endings
forgot ourselves
for the coming cold
summer gone and
dropped somewhere
behind

when a thing like that
is lost we should find it
nothing left to lose
but grief
and in its place
remembrance
and the promise
of sky

Out

in dark times
eye can always see
a way out

use open palms
to divide
the reeds

and emerge
new
and alive

II.

Thundersnow

believe if you want
the low rumble above

to be the result of some god
hurling worlds together

in torment or fury
it would be easy

when the gray-draped sky
flares like candles

lit inside a murky hall
below where we watch

the sky in storm is worth our pause
there are things in nature

we rarely see despite hearing
stories and when at last we do

no matter for god or thunder
reverence is reverence

OUTAGE

when the power went out
it left behind thoughts of thoreau
when he passed through
concord on a snowy walk and paused
to note two thin paths
on either side of the street
made by his neighbors and used
to move from place to place
he laughed to see
and not without contempt
how bound they were to ease
no footprints anywhere else
but those straight lines
later in his diary he wrote
a short lament for his town in snow
a milky landscape undisturbed
told him no one was exploring
the bright world changed
it's not as if his voice
reached me here and yet
when the power went out
he sprang to mind
some signal nearly lost to time
brought the slightest twinge

not of regret or frustration
but hopeful adventure and
paths unknown

CLARITY

eye can see everything
with perfect clarity

as if it happened yesterday
or last night

eye can see a mother
flattened

on the bedroom floor
not awake and not asleep

downstairs in the kitchen
a dog whines

above an empty bowl
and the faucet runs and runs

what has she been doing
all day

driving and drinking
weeping and sleeping

past is dead
here in the present

eye can't drink
eye can't sleep

but eye can weep
and will

Mice in the Attic

they scratched us awake
at midnight directly overhead

was the bait up there not working
and was it too late to check
or wage some violent cleansing
of poison or fire

and where were they entering
how did they get up there
we asked because last fall we'd sealed
every hole we could see

and the question itself bore
the inescapable truth
the difference was
the holes we couldn't see

we remembered then

regardless of resistance
and despite the traps we set
whatever is out
will always come in

TREE

in 82 or 83 when
mom was in rehab
dad realized
it was halloween
and something
normal was crucial so
he found my brown
coat and we collected
wide leaves fallen
from the big maple
here he said
pinning them on
now you are a tree
and for the last he found
a greeting card of
a spooky cartoon oak
someone sent
just days before and cut
two holes
tied some string
and put it on my face
you are a tree he said
and in the dark
we went from

house to house
hand in hand
and took
what we were
given

Spin Cycle

the consequence of lovemaking
with a half-drafted poem

in mind is nearly the same
as overloading the washer

by the time it hits spin
there's too much entropy

sodden motion and a hefty jolt
pops open the door until

there they are all spilled out
your trusty pair

of spotted socks your
corduroys and button-up

all wet very wet
and weighty

but clean so clean
though not yet finished

Walking at Night

after dark
late

other people's rooms
seen from the street
through windows

and what is happening here
in this little glowing box
one sits at a table alone
the other
is in a different room
with a book

wars of silence
are fought at night

the soldiers grow
fatigued while we
civilians nervously
wait to be
called up

ANXIETY IN GENERAL

take it   make

it stop   this must be

what it's like

to be

helpless

beneath a mound

of snow   no place

to grip or grasp

each swiping handful

only digging deeper

and yes

it's like a death

of the present

and a wrenching into

future and   past

where

          somehow

you live

simultaneously panicked

over wrong things

said and done   chances

missed or

events unknown but

already planned   by

a mind in desperation

no one sees   no one

knows by looking

the cracks and swells

of thought and fear

first here   then there

          then there

then here

and talking is   no

solution   because

stories are too real

and lived again

in a calamitous spiral

of   weight pushing you

ever under

          underneath light

and safety   until

all you want

        desire

and yearn for

is   sleep

dark sweetness

and   relief

knowing

you lasted   another

twelve hours

and though you'd fight

        like hell

not to have to do it

tomorrow

you know

with your last grain

of self-compassion

you know

when it comes to it

and it will

you can

Buried / Unburied

panic when
the snowplow
buries the mailbox

how will we get
messages if
there's nowhere
to put them

so that's what
we unbury first
each heft of snow
a pledge
we can again have our
paper dreams and news

when it's done
relief

not of knowing
we'll receive
a specific set of hopes

something
better instead

the possibility
they'll soon
arrive

While Hiking the Flatirons

this
you said
pointing to
a pearl of scar
just above your wrist
in response
to whether
your accident
left any more pain

when it disappeared
you said
you'd finally be
without visible
reminder
each time you
held a pen or
tied a shoe
but not
you said
without of course
the inner scar
a wound of silence

above us
just then
on the limb of a fir
a magpie screeched
and fell into
flight

THE STORM'S END IS COMPARED TO A DEATH

in that we stayed inside
for a long while
warm and comfortable
in familiar bodies until
slowly the snow eased
the threshold was
unburdened and we pushed
aside mounded heaps
to move into the open
under a clearing sky
on our way elsewhere

EMPTY CHURCHES

churches are lovely
when empty
when empty of us

or empty except for
one of us
who heard the bell
who wandered in
from the blizzard
put eyes on the arches
and sat in the dim
stained light of those
windows

if you want to learn
what wonder is

find an empty church
and leave it

A Boy Implores

eye of god
please
turn to me
to see and hear
to heal
my mother
and in your infinite gaze
reverse time
oh eye
before my birth
to hers and make
that subtle change
some small
quietness
inserted at the start
that would instead
lead to
a now of me
asleep
serene
and not this
slipshod begging
in the weepy shape
of some
poor stuttered
prayer

This Poem Isn't Going to Write Itself

can you imagine
all the poets

working on a still morning
like this

their families move
through rooms

close by
and outside

the snow needs clearing
but

try telling that to
a mind in fever

hot and pumping
quietly so

quietly

First Loss

my brother doesn't know
what the leaves were doing
hanging still or shaking
just that it was sunny
as it often is in fall

he remembers finding the old man
slumped on his porch
my brother passing
with a wheelbarrow of brush
for the gully until
something was off he thought
and raced home
brought my father back
who laid the man flat
and pounded his chest
and called his name
and gave instructions
my brother followed
but they knew without saying
there was no more to do

that part has been told
and retold
but what happened after
my brother just twelve
unaccustomed to endings
what did he feel
when he watched my father
pound and yell and pound
but lose
not his last loss
he'd lose again
but there on the porch
what did he say
of my brother's first

my brother can't remember
so many years on
but we agree
maybe thank you
you did well
or look just there look
how bright are those
leaves and what a beautiful
day a bright and warm day
don't be afraid
what comfort it is
to have a day
like this to die

EYE OF THE STORM

stuck for hours
within walls
you're finally tired of stillness
and go outside
in the storm where
you're caught off guard
pummeled by a special
darkness in a night
absent of moon
thirty steps into the drifts
and you just can't say
where the street begins
and the driveway ends
the lights of nearby houses
unknowable behind
a screen of heavy snow
you've heard the tales
of those who ditch maps
to get lost on purpose
driving to rural towns
or distant cities to feel
the sweet renewal of
disorientation
who knew you'd join them

in the storm where
you can only see in snippets
but note that beating
in your chest
that rise and fall of breath
that icy roar of night dissolving
rejoice and revel
claim this rapture
if you'd stayed inside
you'd have missed
this precious gift
of sight

Montaigne

what he wanted was
to sit alone in that tower
and know peace

what he discovered was
the mind
moves always

just like the river
where a certain length
of water appears static

until the eye
understands infinity
in microscopic

elements bound
by perpetual flow
and tumble

he wrote and wrote
wrestled to keep
his mind

subdued
and we know
the rest

if we've read
his books
his beautiful

rhapsodies
that never
stop going

III.

Eye of the Mind

eye of the mind
is a memory filter
viewer of past events
and knower of
very little for sure

what can eye see
eye of the mind
collector of dangerous
objects and watcher
of intimate histories

losses and fears
are dangerous objects
eye of the mind
observes and records
watch out says eye

and watch in as well
what happened outside
will happen within
eye of the mind
can forget it there

but never forget
the lovely things
the things that
weave your joy warns
eye of the mind

In a Box of Old Toys

what do we owe the children
we were
what kind of life

in a box of old toys
race cars rest with
a mustache and glasses
and a slim plastic lion

if we tried would we
still know how to imagine

even if we don't
those children do
they sing out in times of silence
a chorus of remembrance

you've done half your duty
which was to persist
now finish the rest
and come back to us

CANNONBALL

not since you were small
have you rested like this
on your back on the floor
staring at the ceiling until
the world there flips
and your eye takes you
strolling around upside down
dodging ceiling fans and
chandeliers on your way
to a ramp where you slide
with stairs overhead
and launch out a window
cannonballing down
to the clouds

CEMETERY IN WINTER

nothing to it now
except the stones

with hoods of snow
no one visits today

but the dry wind
making little sound

other than
the errant bird

it carries through
and here and there

the clatter of souls

Night Manager

after the plows came
we drove to get milkshakes
we pulled around to the window
where we could see him
careening between counters
disheveled and sweating and
nearly breathless because
as we only realized later
he was alone
the others having stayed
home in the storm
we watched his feet sweep
a pile of loose receipts
and kick some tumbled cups
until he arrived back with us
to collect money and hand over
the goods with a pained smile
the kids may not have known
he was glorious but
of course that's what we are
if despite everything we do our jobs
so the machine continues to run
so it doesn't suddenly
grind and falter leaving us

helpless and stranded
some snowy night
with all the lights on
the equipment squealing
and no one there
to help

WHO'S THERE?

it's impossible to forget
the first line of hamlet
because the who
is the ghost of his dead father

at first this is disturbing
until your own father is
dead and you realize how
wonderful it would be

to see him gliding your way
from some great distance
with arms open wide
so happy to see you

hoping you'll remember
he is the answer
to a desperate question
you asked so long ago

CLEAN DARK

snow
emits light

a special kind
after much has
fallen

even at night
it does

bathing in it
you'll believe

darkness too
emits
light

What Doesn't Break You Makes You Stronger

next month

this heavy snow
pulling down the limbs
of pines

will melt

become water
the trees
will use to
nourish themselves

which just goes
to show you

Don't Make Any Major Decisions in March

is what you said
and we laughed because
we were younger then

we know now
in new england no one's
young for long

friends and pets go
some forever
and bare branches leave

too much space where
the snows of living
fall and fill

deep in the cities
long-faced walkers
stalk dim streets

and in the north
it's the same for farmers
in brittle fields

thirty-one days of
cautious indecision
seems a small price

we all make better
choices in the sun

Lifetime of Things

after their split
my mother moved
out my father stayed
in the house
retired by then he still
visited old patients
got together with
other doctors for lunch
and at night
alone in the house
took photos of
chairs
and carpets
and dishes
preparing
for divorce
compiling
a catalog
of loss

Warming Hours

snowman is us
starting off with
strong stick-arms
lifted high
and bright mouth-stones
glinting until
tomorrow's warmth
sees us listing
little by little
arms sliding down
and our melted smile
popping off
tooth by
sunlit tooth

Winter Thinks of Spring

gradually the landscape reemerges

ice gives way to blacktop and stone
dead leaves are memories of autumn

living here means accepting
both worlds

one of everwhite snow-scrim and things lost
the other underneath all that

hidden for months and then
just when we need it most

when we can't take any more

      becoming alive

Painted Tigers

the zen monk who
painted a tiger

so lifelike
he cowered with fear
learned

what
eye see

creating movement

between
real and imagined

and making them
same

to become
so easily
afraid like

a painted tiger
unmoving

but ready
forever
to pounce

eye
make truth
eye
must
take care

when passing
a tiger
to stay distant
but not far
and never
look

too close

PUSH START

old volkswagens
are much a mirror
for a certain way of
life lived well yet
unpredictable at best
if stalled don't worry
find room and a hill
find neutral
push to speed dive in
drop to second
pop the clutch
slam the gas
hold on and
drive like hell

Snow

one easy metaphor
is that there is also snow within
piling near the eaves
and clogging the walkway
then it melts
and falls again and
we know this as rhythm

why so hard to believe
when snow goes
it will come back
difficult to know
other than that's the way
it is and this is
where you are

Momentary Quiet

because so many of us
are large and loud
my intent at day's end
was to become
small and quiet
alone in a dim room
the only sound was breath
my own
and gradually it began
with slow out and in
to hold every part of
my attention my thoughts
fell so far into breath
the source of life
my intent too fell away
until nothing
remained not intent
or its opposite just
nothing and nothing
had changed
downstairs after joining
my family at the table
our talk was everywhere
and the sound of dishes

and the dog lapping his bowl
but underneath it all
still remembered
was my breath
still breath
still

Visit the Creek in Winter

you won't have to go
far to find the creek
beyond the trees
a hill a path
through new snow
takes you to the edge
where ice clings
to the bank
if you look down
just here
aim an eye at the water
and through it
you can see the silt
bottom beneath
and once or twice
a pebble
an ancient jewel
or the innermost part
of your very own
self
the part
you swore
you'd never lose

These poems were written over five days immediately before, during, and after the last major snowstorm of the year.

Thank you to Samaa Abdurraqib, Ken Craft, Judy Kaber, Jefferson Navicky, Betsy Sholl, Dave Stankiewicz, and everyone at Spuyten Duyvil.

Author photo by Cohen Bove.

MIKE BOVE is the author of three additional poetry collections: *Soundtrack to Your Next Panic Attack* (forthcoming 2024), *House Museum* (2021) and *Big Little City* (2018). His work has appeared in journals in the US, UK, and Canada. He was winner of the 2021 Maine Postmark Poetry Contest and a 2023 finalist for a Maine Literary Award in poetry. He is Professor of English at Southern Maine Community College and lives with his family in Portland, Maine where he was born and raised.

Made in the USA
Middletown, DE
08 September 2023

37657555R00061